DEDICATION

Once again I am reminded of the
deep value of friendship in my life.
I am so blessed and grateful beyond
words to all of you who have
encouraged me and helped me
along this path in every way—
emotionally, spiritually,
and sometimes even financially.
I couldn't possibly list all of
you here—but you know who
you are, and, from the bottom
of my heart, I thank you
for sharing your hearts with me!
May the Lord bless you as much
as you have blessed me.

Sharing Hearts,
a title in the Tea Ladies Collection™
Text © 2001 by Dee Appel,
Published by Blue Cottage Gifts™,
a division of Multnomah Publishers, Inc.®
P.O. Box 1720, Sisters, OR 97759

ISBN: 1-58860-030-0

Artwork designs by Gay Talbott Boassy are
reproduced under license from Indigo Gate and may
not be Reproduced without permission. For more
Information reguarding art featured in this book,
please contact:

> *Mr. Gifford B. Bowne II*
> *Indigo Gate Inc.*
> *1 Pegasus Drive*
> *Colts Neck, NJ 07722*
> *(732) 577– 9333*

Designed by Koechel Peterson & Associates,
Minneapolis, MN

Scripture quotations are taken from *The Holy Bible*,
King James Version; *The Holy Bible*, New
International Version (NIV) ©1973, 1984 by
International Bible Society, used by permission of
Zondervan Publishing House. *The Living Bible* (TLB)
©1971. Used by permision of Tyndale House
Publishers, Inc. All rights reserved.

Printed in China

www.bluecottagegifts.com

Sharing Hearts

LITTLE CHATS for a SWEET LIFE

Written by DEE APPEL

Illustrated by GAY TALBOTT BOASSY

Tea Ladies COLLECTION

Friends can teach us many things,
They offer different views.
They help us see just who we are…
Sometimes with hefty clues!
They ride the tides of joy and loss,
Encourage us to dream…
They make life fun and give us hope,
They boost our self-esteem.
They're known for bringing out our best,
Or worst, as fate would have it—
They bind our wounded hearts with love,
Or what it takes to salve it.
We build our trust and faith in them,
And that is where it starts.
It grows into a lovely thing
When friends can share their hearts.

FRIENDS…

THEY ARE

KIND

TO EACH

OTHER'S

HOPES,

THEY

CHERISH

EACH

OTHER'S

DREAMS.

HENRY DAVID THOREAU

The BEGINNING

One night we had a sleepover—
We thought it would be great.
Minty's was the perfect place,
And so we met at eight.

Darjie brought some
strange hors d'oeuvres
That none of us had seen.
They looked like eyeballs for a start,
And even Jazz turned green!

Darjie was a good sport, though,
When each of us declined
To try her high-end dainty dish,
We said, "It's too refined!"

FRIENDS ARE
LIKE ANGELS
WHO LIFT US TO
OUR FEET
WHEN OUR
WINGS
HAVE
TROUBLE
REMEMBERING
HOW TO FLY.

ANONYMOUS

We all put on our pj's,

And it was quite a sight—

From Minty's red-and-

white striped shirt

To Darjie's lace delight!

Conversation turned to life—

From fat and weight to aging,

To money with its

highs and lows—

The topics were amazing!

When friends take time

to have some fun,

Learn from each other's lives,

You'd be surprised

how much there is

And how the time just flies!

The night went on and on it seemed

As hours passed us by.

We ate until we'd

stuffed ourselves

And laughed until we cried.

IT IS ONE
OF THE
BLESSINGS
OF OLD
FRIENDS
THAT
YOU CAN
AFFORD
TO BE
STUPID
WITH
THEM.

RALPH WALDO EMERSON

ORANGE PEKOE

OPIE TEACHES LAUGHTER IS THE BEST MEDICINE

Orange Pekoe was just so pleased

To get to be with us,

She shared that she would

soon start school

And ride there on the bus!

She's so darned cute, we all agreed,

And life for her's so simple…

Wasn't it just weeks ago

Big worries meant a pimple?

Opie may be slightly shy,

But she does not miss much.

We get the biggest

kicks from her,

And she keeps us all in touch

With that childlike side of us,

Which we tend to forget.

She's happy to remind us all

That laughing's

our best bet!

A MERRY HEART DOETH GOOD LIKE A MEDICINE...

PROVERBS 17:22

Her life seems so effortless
At her tender age.
It's a bit more of an effort
By the time you are a sage!
When Pekoe said,
"It's time for bed,"
And Opie said "good night,"
She kissed us all before she left—
That child brings such delight!

WE EACH
SHOULD
TAKE A
LESSON
FROM
THE
CHILDREN
IN OUR
LIVES.
JOY AND
LAUGHTER
ARE THE
THINGS
ON WHICH
THE HEART
THRIVES.

PEKOE —
THE ART
OF AGING

Pekoe is a marvel.

We have all agreed

That she is simply ageless...

"Please tell us how," we plead!

"Age is really just the way

You think about yourself.

It's not to do with tons of creams

Sitting on your shelf.

If you 'think young'

And take good care

With rest and exercise,
Eat lots of fruits and veggies, too,
And cut out those french fries!
I've learned that life is kind to you
If you are kind to it.
Take the time to care for you
And age won't hurt a bit!
You need to slow the tempo down
And when you're young, it's hard,
But take a break, and take a walk,
Or pull weeds in your yard.
You'll be surprised how good it feels
If you heed my advice.
You may find that aging is,
In some ways, even nice.

IS NOT WISDOM FOUND AMONG THE AGED?

JOB 12:12

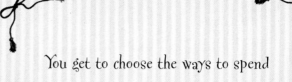

You get to choose the ways to spend
Your days from morn 'til night.
You can read a book all day,
Which I find a delight.
You'll see things differently with time,
And wisdom comes with years.
If you learn now—look through my eyes,
And that should calm your fears".

BEING A
GRAND-
MOTHER
MEANS
GETTING
THE
OPPORTUNITY
TO DO
IT ALL
OVER
AGAIN,
ONLY
BETTER.

PEKOE

JAZZIE
ON CELLULITE

Jazzie simply loves to eat
Everything in sight,
And she is also first to say
She knows it isn't right.
She eats because she's happy,
She eats because she's sad,
She eats because it's time to—
It's really gotten bad!
"It truly is a curse, I know—
And I must change my ways,
Or else I know that there will be
A weighty price to pay!

JASMINE

It's time to think of salads

       And eating balanced meals.

The times I do, I'm happier

       And I like the way I feel.

I'm so hooked on carbs, I know

       If I don't get it right,

I'm doomed to life of sporting thighs

       Full of cellulite!"

Salad

Jazz admits that she would like

To find a guy to wed,

But first she needs to love herself,

And that is what we said.

Each of us has to learn

That no one else can do it…

Only we can change our ways,

And we'd better get right to it!

DEAR

FRIEND,

I PRAY

THAT

YOU

MAY

ENJOY

GOOD

HEALTH....

PROVERBS 27:9

MINTY—LIFE IS A CHOICE

Jazz asked Minty if she missed
The life she used to lead.
She was on a path in her career
That would certainly succeed.
She had been an editor
For a well-known magazine.
Her natural way with food and style
Made her the Edit Queen!
"There are times I do look back,"
Minty said to Jazz.
"That flashy life I left behind
Was fun and had pizzazz.

PEPPERMINT

DON'T BE SOMEONE YOU ARE NOT,
THEIR SKIN WON'T FIT ON YOU.
JUST BE THE BEST
OF WHO YOU ARE AND
LET YOUR LOVE
SHINE THROUGH.

But I wouldn't trade it for the world—
My married life is bliss.
Who could ask for any more…
My day starts with a kiss!
I can't wait 'til children come,
And for that day I pray.
Meanwhile, I am very blessed
In the life I lead today."
Darjie asked the secret of
Her joyful, happy ways.
Minty smiled and told us that
It boils down to this phrase:

"Life is full of choices and
We're the ones who choose,
It's all in how we look at things
That makes us win or lose.
The cup can be half empty
Or it can be half full…
The door can open either way
We can choose to push or pull.
No matter how we cut the cake,
We're the ones to slice it…
You can pick a great big piece
Or make a choice to dice it!"

FRIENDS

ARE

THE

GOOD

LORD'S

WAY OF

TAKING

CARE

OF US.

DARJIE

DARJEELING

A HOT FLASH
FROM DARJIE

Darjie seemed a little tired,
Without her usual zip,
And there was barely any hint
Of lipstick on her lips!
We asked her if she felt okay,
And she let out a sigh.
We knew that there was something wrong
When she began to cry.
"I've not been sleeping well at all,"
She started to explain.
"I toss and turn with hot and cold—
I feel like I'm insane!

REAL FRIENDS
ARE THOSE WHO,
WHEN YOU FEEL
YOU'VE MADE
A FOOL OF
YOURSELF,
DON'T FEEL
YOU'VE DONE
A PERMANENT JOB.

And when I'm riding in my car

I drive poor Murphy mad.

He has to keep the cool air on—

It's really getting bad!

I just can't stand

the thought of it,

My skin is full of flaws.

I can't control

emotions now—

It's really

menopause!"

We hastened to assure our friend
That it was just a stage,
That each of us would feel this way
When we hit a certain age.
Darjie seemed relieved to see
We'd love her anyway.
She thanked us all for putting up
With how she felt today.
Jazzie somehow changed the mood
When she said something funny,
And then the topic took a turn—
The subject now was money.
Cammie meant no harm, of course,
When she asked for advice—
"Darjie, what's it like to shop
And not look at the price?"

KIND WORDS ARE LIKE HONEY, ENJOYABLE AND HEALTHY.

PROVERBS 16:24

We were all a little stunned,
And held our breath to see
If Darjie would get mad at her
And just get up and leave.
To our relief she laughed and said,
"My dear, I hope you know
That money can't buy love nor friends
And often brings great woe.
Sure, it's nice to have nice things
And travel now and then,
But nothing on this earth is as
Important as a friend.
You are all so dear to me
I can't even tell you, honey.
You love me just for who I am
And not for all my money."

About that time Strudle made
A beeline for the door.
Darjie grabbed his leash and said
That she'd be back for more.

COUNT

YOUR

AGE

WITH

FRIENDS

BUT

NOT

WITH

YEARS.

ANONYMOUS

CHAMOMILE

CAMMIE—THE JOYS OF SOLITUDE

Cammie lives alone, you know,
And she is first to say
That she enjoys her solitude
In every single way.
We asked her how she does it…
"It doesn't drive me crazy—
Sometimes I fill up my day
Being absolutely lazy.
I take a long, hot bubble bath
Or write a friend a letter.
I read a book or magazine
Or walk my Irish setter.

EVEN IF YOU'RE BROKE

AND HAVEN'T GOT A PENNY,

YOU CAN ALWAYS

GIVE A HUG

TO ONE WHO

HASN'T ANY.

CAMMIE

I've signed up for a class or two...
My favorite one is art.
I'm certainly not good at it,
But it's a place to start."
Darjie razzed her just a bit,
"I bet you'd keep them hopping
If you'd suggest they let you teach
A class called 'Art of Shopping!'"
Cammie took it all in fun—
She didn't mind a bit,
And promised she would call the school
And look right into it.
We're all grateful for the love
She gives from her sweet heart,
And listening to her friends in need
Is her perfected art.

We're convinced we'd wear her out,

But she knows how to be

A happy camper on her own—

The perfect company!

She fills her cup by taking care

Of her own soul and mind...

She pours it back on us in love

Of the sweetest kind.

KIND
HEARTS
ARE THE
GARDENS,
KIND
THOUGHTS
ARE THE
SEEDS,
KIND
WORDS
ARE THE
BLOSSOMS,
THE
FRUITS
ARE KIND
DEEDS.

SARA AGE 7 1902

We still meet on Sundays
At the willow tree.
We find that there is nothing like
An afternoon of tea.
We highly recommend to you
That you take time to sup.
Sharing hearts with those you love
Will always fill your cup!

A FRIEND IS A PERSON
WITH WHOM
I MAY BE SINCERE.
BEFORE HIM,
I MAY THINK ALOUD.

RALPH WALDO EMERSON